PEOPLE WHO MADE HISTORY
NATIVE AMERICANS

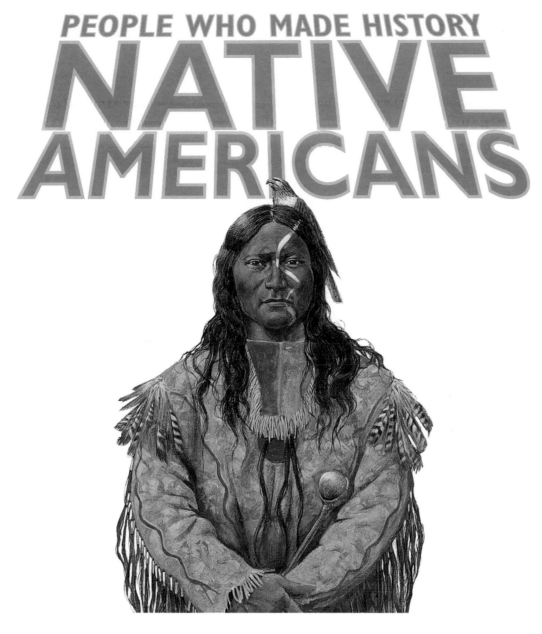

by Jason Hook
Illustrated by Richard Hook

RAINTREE
STECK-VAUGHN
PUBLISHERS

A Harcourt Company

Austin   New York
www.steck-vaughn.com

Picture acknowledgments

The publisher would like to thank the following for their kind permission to use these pictures: Bridgeman 6, 8, 9, 10, 12, 13, 21 (left), 26, 41 (above); Eye Ubiquitous 14; Hodder/ Wayland 18, 43; Hulton Getty 22, 28, 30, (H. H. Clarke) 33, (John C. H. Grabill) 38, (D. F. Barns) 40; John Frost Historical Newspapers 37; Mary Evans Picture Library 17; Peter Newark's Pictures 5, 16, 21 (right), 37, 41 (below), 43; Photri 20, 25, (Maj Vee Moorhouse) 29; Stockmarket 42; Topham Picturepoint *cover*, 24, 32, 34; Werner Forman Archive 36.

The maps on pages 4 and 22 are by Peter Bull.

People who made history

Ancient Greece • Ancient Egypt • Ancient Rome • Native Americans

Published by Raintree Steck-Vaughn Publishers, an imprint of Steck-Vaughn Company

Library of Congress Cataloging-in-Publication Data
Hook, Jason.
Native Americans / Jason Hook; illustrated by Richard Hook.
    p.   cm.—(People who made history)
    Includes bibliographical references and index.
    ISBN 0-7398-2750-2
    1. Indians of North America—Biography—Juvenile literature.
    2. Indian women—North America—Biography—Juvenile literature.
    [1. Indians of North America—Biography.]
    I. Hook, Richard, ill. II. Title. III. People who made history.
    E89.H662 2000
    970.004'97'00922—dc21   00-031076

Printed in Italy. Bound in the United States.
1 2 3 4 5 6 7 8 9 0 05 04 03 02 01

Contents

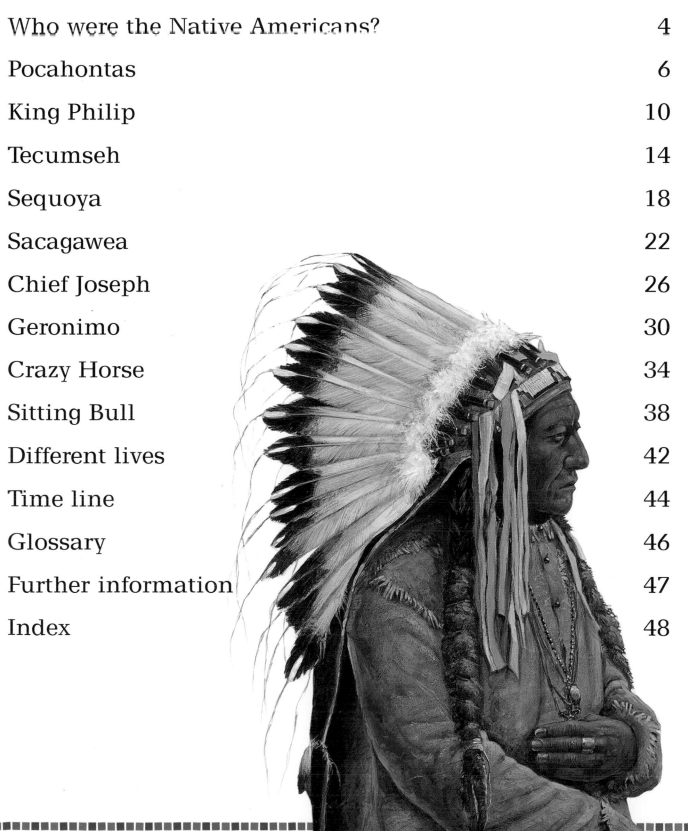

Who were the Native Americans?   4

Pocahontas   6

King Philip   10

Tecumseh   14

Sequoya   18

Sacagawea   22

Chief Joseph   26

Geronimo   30

Crazy Horse   34

Sitting Bull   38

Different lives   42

Time line   44

Glossary   46

Further information   47

Index   48

Who were the Native Americans?

THE MISUNDERSTANDINGS between the Native Americans and the Europeans began as soon as Christopher Columbus stepped ashore in the Caribbean on October 12, 1492. He had come searching for the silk, spices, and other treasures of the East. Mistakenly believing that he had reached the East Indies (Southeast Asia), Columbus called the people he found there "Indians."

Although Columbus claimed to have "discovered" America, the Native Americans had actually lived on this continent since about 12,000 B.C. They were not a single nation, but a

▼ A map of North America showing the traditional homelands of the nations and peoples described in this book

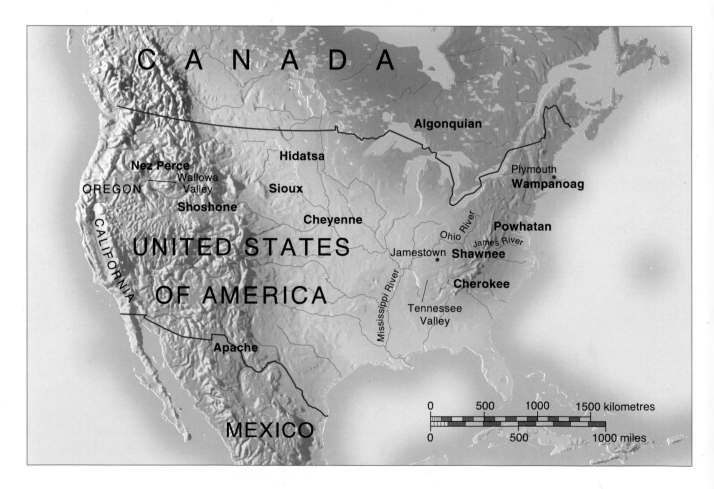

► The Native Americans had their own cultures before the Europeans arrived. This painting from 1585 shows a village with reed houses, planted fields, and men performing a sacred dance.

rich variety of peoples, languages, and cultures. The Europeans spoke of them as "heathens" because they were not Christian. In fact, the Native Americans had their own religions, including beautiful creation myths that told how the Sacred Powers had first given them the land.

Indian nations had historians who could describe all the important events in their people's long history. But they had no form of writing. Most of our knowledge of Native Americans comes from the writing of European settlers. So, the most famous Indians are those who played a part in the history of the settlers. There were other Native Americans who were legendary among their own people long before the Europeans arrived—we just don't know as much about their lives.

In most Native American societies, chiefs were simply people of influence. They could speak only for those small groups of their people who chose to follow them. To the Europeans, chiefs were kings or rulers who could touch a pen to a treaty and sign away their people's lands. This misunderstanding was to cause many problems in the years to come.

Native Americans in the time of Pocahontas

IN APRIL 1607, three ships sailed up the James River on America's Northeast coast. Onboard were 104 settlers. They would found England's first successful colony in North America—Jamestown, Virginia. The people who lived beside the river watched the towering masts drift through their homeland waters. They called the strange arrivals "Coat-Wearers."

The English settlers came from a country of growing cities, fashionable clothes, iron and gunpowder, pounds and shillings, Christian worship, and Shakespearean plays. The people they now met lived in bark-covered huts, wore breechcloths of deerskin, farmed with tools of bone, used shells for money, and worshiped powerful nature spirits.

The colonists survived only because these "Indians" traded them corn for metal axes and glass beads. This peaceful trade did not last. Armed with muskets, Captain John Smith led expeditions from Jamestown into the dense woodlands to take corn by force. His fate, and that of the colony, would depend on a thirteen-year-old girl named Pocahontas.

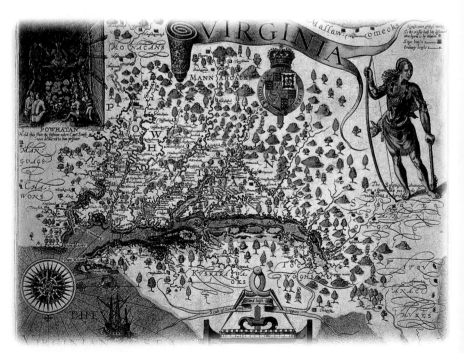

► A map of Virginia made by John Smith, a leader of the Jamestown colony

POCAHONTAS

Daughter of Powhatan
circa 1595 to 1617

On one expedition, Smith was captured and taken to the village of the most powerful chief in the region, 60-year-old Powhatan. According to Smith's diary, the chief sentenced him to death. But as warriors raised their war clubs, Powhatan's daughter Pocahontas rushed forward to beg for Smith's life. Her father let him live. This tale created the legend of Pocahontas, who became a symbol of friendship between the Native Americans and the English.

LANGUAGE

Pocahontas's people belonged to a group of Native Americans that spoke a family of languages called Algonquian. From their languages we get words such as moccasin, papoose, squaw, and wigwam.

Powhatan now agreed to trade with Jamestown, and Pocahontas started visiting the settlement. Smith wrote: "Blessed Pocahontas, the great king's daughter of Virginia, oft saved my life . . . [and] was the instrument to preserve this colony from death, famine, and confusion."

◄ As a captive in Jamestown, Pocahontas began to adopt English customs. She learned to behave, speak, and dress in the English way.

SPOTLIGHT ON POCAHONTAS

Indian Name:	Matoaka—which means "she has fun playing"
Nickname:	Pocahontas—which means "frisky"
English Name:	Lady Rebecca—given to her when she was baptized
People:	Powhatan (named by the Europeans after Pocahontas's father)
Position:	Daughter of Chief Powhatan
Born:	About 1595, Virginia, near James River
Died:	1617, Gravesend, England
They Said:	"Her great appearance of love to me is her desire to be taught and instructed in the knowledge of God." (John Rolfe, 1614)

More settlers began to arrive, and English commanders tried to reduce Powhatan's power by burning Indian villages and even kidnapping and murdering the children of local chiefs. In 1613, Pocahontas was herself taken hostage.

Pocahontas Among the English

Pocahontas was held captive at Jamestown for a year. At first, she shocked the people there. She expressed her joyful nature by turning cartwheels naked! Slowly, though, she learned to speak and behave in the English way. She became the first of her people to be baptized. Finally, she married an English settler named John Rolfe. The marriage secured peace between Powhatan and the settlers. Rolfe also learned to grow an important Indian crop—tobacco.

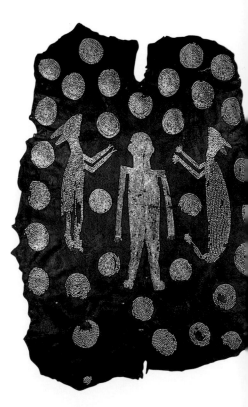

► Powhatan's cloak, used for ceremonies. It was made of deerskin and decorated with thousands of shell beads.

In 1616, Pocahontas sailed to England with her husband, their new son, Thomas, and ten Indian leaders. In London, she met King James I and the famous playwright Ben Jonson. But before Pocahontas could carry such tales back to America, she caught smallpox. In March 1617, she died.

The life of Pocahontas could have served as a warning to the Native Americans. Missionaries arrived to preach the Christian religion she had adopted. Her husband's tobacco crop was sold to England, and thousands more settlers arrived to share in Jamestown's wealth. They carried diseases such as smallpox and measles, and whole villages of Pocahontas's people died the way she did. The Coat-Wearers were there to stay.

▲ This engraving of Pocahontas shows how she looked in European costume when she visited England.

SQUANTO

Pocahontas was not the only Native American to help a colony survive. When the Pilgrim Fathers landed at Plymouth in 1620, they were amazed to find help from a Wampanoag Indian, called Squanto, who spoke English. He had learned the language when kidnapped by sailors.

Native Americans in the Time of King Philip

WHEN THEY traded with the first settlers, the native people could not imagine how many more would soon follow. Powhatan had asked a chief who traveled to England with Pocahontas to count the population by making notches on a stick. The chief was said to have grown "weary of the task."

In 1621, Squanto, the Wampanoag who had befriended the Pilgrim Fathers, arranged a treaty of friendship between his people and the settlers of the new Plymouth colony. It was signed by Massasoit, the sachem, or great chief, of the Wampanoag. Massasoit kept this peace, even as 50,000 settlers flooded into his homeland.

These settlers brought missionaries, who persuaded some Indians to become Christians and to go live like Europeans in new "praying towns." Settlers also brought alcohol and sold it to Indians in return for agreements to give away their land. When Massasoit died in 1661, his son, King Philip, realized that his people's whole way of life was under threat.

CHIEFS

Native Americans had many different kinds of chiefs. The Wampanoags were led by a tribal sachem who advised several village sachems. Although this position could be passed from father to son, a poor sachem soon lost his followers. One colonist noted "how powerful the kings are, and yet how they move by the breath of the people." Although most chiefs were men, the widow of Philip's brother, Wetamoo, was a leader in Philip's war. She became known as the "Squaw Sachem."

KING PHILIP

Chief of the Wampanoag
circa 1638 to 1676

There were hundreds of Native American nations. Each one fought wars, made treaties, and traded with its neighbors. When one of these nations went to war with the Europeans, the settlers brutally defeated them using guns, and they often wiped out whole communities. King Philip was the first chief to see that only a united force of many Indian nations could stop the Europeans from taking more of their land.

▼ King Philip, wearing a cloak, wampum headband, war paint, and earrings of swansdown. He is carrying his ball-headed war club.

King Philip was twenty-four when he became grand sachem of the Wampanoag. He complained about the praying towns, telling one missionary that he cared as much for Christianity as for a button on the man's coat. Philip also argued that Indians should not have to follow laws invented by the leaders of the Plymouth colony.

The Plymouth leaders accused Philip of "behaving insolently [rudely] and proudly towards us on several occasions." In 1671, they forced him to sign a treaty, promising never to sell land without the permission of the Plymouth colony. Relations between King Philip and the Plymouth colony grew worse as the settlers demanded more land. Finally, war broke out.

◄ In New England, belts of white and purple shell beads, or wampum, were used to send messages of war or friendship.

SPOTLIGHT ON KING PHILIP

Name: Metacom or Metacomet

English Name: King Philip. At Massasoit's request, the Plymouth leaders gave his two sons English names—they were named after Alexander the Great and Philip II of Macedon.

People: Wampanoag

Position: Sachem

Born: About 1638, near Pokanoket, Massachusetts

Died: 1676, Pokanoket

They Said: "'They did roar against us like so many wild bulls." (A settler writing about attacks by Philip's warriors, 1675)

King Philip's War

In 1675, King Philip's War began. Warriors from the Wampanoag, Narragansett, and Nipmuck peoples joined the attacks. For a year, fighting raged through New England, the area settled by Europeans. The Indians attacked 52 of the 90 settlements. They destroyed 12 of them, killing 600 settlers and coming within a mile or so of Plymouth.

But not all the Indians joined Philip's alliance. The Mohawk and Mohegan nations, and Indians from the praying towns, fought on the side of the English. Then a band of Wampanoags betrayed Philip, leading English troops to his camp. They killed 173 of his people and captured his wife and son—who were sent to the West Indies as slaves. Philip escaped, but said: "My heart breaks. Now I am ready to die." He returned to the village of his birth, where in August 1676, he was ambushed and killed.

▲ King Philip's followers were ferocious fighters. Many Native Americans in this region fought with carved, ball-headed clubs like this one.

12

Philip's head was cut off and displayed on a pole at Plymouth for the next twenty years. The Wampanoag man who had betrayed him cut off Philip's hand and kept it preserved in a bucket of rum. He showed it to settlers in exchange for gifts. It was a fitting symbol. Philip had fought to stop his people from selling their land for alcohol. He failed because some of his own people betrayed him.

PIRATES

In 1676, during King Philip's War, Indians led by a man known as Rogue Mugg made terrifying pirate raids on English ships from canoes. Mugg's pirates captured one English vessel and ransacked a settlement in Maine.

◄ A painting from 1710 showing a chief of the Mohawk—one of the peoples that fought against King Philip. No portrait was ever made of Philip. One portrait often said to be of him was in fact based on this painting.

Native Americans in the time of Tecumseh

"WHERE ARE the Narragansett, the Mahican, the Pokanoket, and many other once powerful tribes of our people? They have vanished before the avarice and oppression [greed and cruel treatment] of the white man, as snow before a summer sun."

The Shawnee leader, Tecumseh, made this speech in 1811. The Narragansett and Pokanoket he spoke of had been all but wiped out during King Philip's War. The Mahicans had sold their lands. Tecumseh's people, the Shawnee, who lived farther west beyond the Ohio River, now found their own future under threat.

In 1768, the year that Tecumseh was born, the British had banned settlers from traveling west of the Ohio River. In 1783, though, the European colonists won their independence from British rule and formed the United States of America. Now there was nothing to stop the American fur traders and settlers from pressing westward into Ohio and Indiana. In his heroic attempts to stop them, Tecumseh would prove himself one of the greatest of all Native Americans.

▼ A total eclipse of the sun was a magical symbol to the Native Americans.

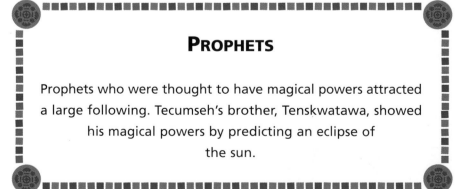

PROPHETS

Prophets who were thought to have magical powers attracted a large following. Tecumseh's brother, Tenskwatawa, showed his magical powers by predicting an eclipse of the sun.

TECUMSEH Chief and orator
circa 1768 to 1813

Like King Philip, Tecumseh saw the need for Indian nations to unite in defense of their land. In his youth, he had seen his father and two brothers killed by the settlers, now known as Americans, and had watched his chiefs sign away much of the Shawnee lands.

Tecumseh was helped by his younger brother. Named Lalawethika, or "Noise Maker," he was best known for getting drunk at American trading posts. Then, in 1805, Lalawethika saw a vision telling him to return to a traditional way of life. He changed his name to Tenskwatawa, or "Open Door," and began preaching. Tecumseh set up a village called Prophet's Town, where a thousand Indians from different tribes gathered around Tenskwatawa.

In 1810, Tecumseh met with William Henry Harrison, the Governor of Indiana Territory who had recently persuaded Native American peoples to sign a treaty giving away 4,600 square miles (12,000 sq km) of land. Tecumseh told Harrison: "No tribe has a right to sell . . . Sell a country! Why not sell the air, the clouds, and the great sea, as well as the earth?"

As the two men sat side by side on a bench, Tecumseh kept sliding along until Harrison had nearly fallen off. When he complained, Tecumseh laughed and explained that this was what the Americans were doing to the Indians.

▼ Tecumseh holding a wampum belt while making a speech. He was said to be a magnificent speaker.

SPOTLIGHT ON TECUMSEH

Indian Name:	Tecumtha—which means "Panther Lying in Wait"
English Name:	Tecumseh
People:	Shawnee
Position:	Chief and speech-maker
Born:	1768, on Mad River, Ohio, in the month the Shawnee called the Moon of Singing Frogs
Died:	1813, Battle of the Thames
They Said:	"One of those uncommon geniuses who spring up occasionally to overturn the established order of things." (William Harrison, 1810)

Fighting the Americans

The following year, Tecumseh made an extraordinary journey. He went north to Canada, to ask the Indian tribes and the British to join his fight against the Americans. He then traveled 1,000 miles (1,600 km) south to what is now Alabama to urge the Native American peoples of the southeast to join him. Everywhere, he lit up Indian villages with his speeches. One observer wrote: "His voice resounded over the multitude—now sinking in low and musical whispers, now rising to the highest key, hurling out his words like a succession of thunderbolts."

As Tecumseh's Indian alliance grew, disaster hit Prophet's Town. While Tecumseh was away, Harrison led an attack on the village. He burned it to the ground, and Tenskwatawa's followers fled in despair.

PONTIAC

Pontiac, a chief of the Ottowa people, led an uprising against the British settlers in 1763. Many peoples in the northeast joined the uprising. They captured eight English forts, including Detroit, before Pontiac was finally defeated.

▲ An engraving of Tecumseh in British uniform, but wearing the traditional turban of the Shawnee.

◄ General William Henry Harrison defeated Tecumseh at the Battle of the Thames, and later became President.

Tecumseh had one last hope of victory. In 1812, the United States went to war against the British in Canada. Tecumseh joined the war on the side of the British, and his alliance of warriors from many Indian peoples won a number of battles. But at the Battle of the Thames in 1813, Tecumseh's dream ended. He was killed fighting against his old enemy General Harrison. He had come as close as any Indian leader to uniting his people, but after his death the westward flood of white settlers could not be stopped.

Native Americans in the time of Sequoyah

SOME NATIVE American peoples were persuaded to adapt to European ways, because they thought it would help them to hold onto their lands. The Cherokee lived in the Tennessee Valley, and were the largest nation in the southeastern United States. They were known for their craftworkers, who made baskets and pottery, and for their healers. By 1829 they had taken up the European style of farming, keeping farm animals. They had blacksmiths, roads, schools, and sawmills. A few Cherokee even ran cotton plantations using black slaves.

Some Native Americans called 1829 the year "the Devil became President." New president Andrew Jackson ignored the fact that the Cherokee had settled like Europeans. In 1830 he passed the Indian Removal Act. This said that all Native Americans had to give up their land to American settlers and move to "Indian Territory" west of the Mississippi.

The Cherokee did not take up arms to resist Jackson. Instead they fought him in the Supreme Court, the highest court in the land! The remarkable invention of a man named Sequoyah helped them to do this.

▼ A traditional Cherokee basket, woven by a skilled craftworker

SEQUOYAH

**Scholar and inventor
circa 1760 to 1843**

Much of what we know about Native Americans comes from the writing of European settlers. The Indians themselves had rich spoken languages and passed on their history by word of mouth. But they had no written alphabet that exactly matched the sounds of their own languages. This changed through the genius of Sequoyah.

Sequoyah did not go to school and could not speak or write English. However, he was a talented painter. When Sequoyah saw a letter stolen from a settler's pocket, he promised to invent his own written alphabet for the Cherokee language.

Sequoyah locked himself away in his cabin and used his painting skills to draw pictures for his words. His people grew suspicious and accused him of being a witch. When they burned down his cabin and all his papers, Sequoyah traveled west to Indian Territory. There, he carried on his lonely work.

◄ Sequoyah writing, wearing a medal given to him later in life by the United States government

A FINE SURRENDER

The Cherokees' neighbors, the Seminole, fought a long war against the Indian Removal Act. Their leader, Osceola, surrendered in 1838. Three chiefs who had stolen a trunk of theater costumes surrendered dressed as Hamlet, Richard III, and Horatio from Shakespeare's plays.

SPOTLIGHT ON SEQUOYAH

Indian Name:	Sequoyah
English Name:	George Gist (His father was a European trader.)
People:	Cherokee
Position:	Scholar, inventor, writer
Born:	About 1760 in Taskigi, Tennessee
Died:	1843, Mexico
They Said:	"With no prompter but his own genius, and no guide but the light of reason, he had formed an alphabet." (Thomas McKenney, Superintendent of Indian Trade, 1836)

Sequoyah's Alphabet

In 1821, after twelve years of study, Sequoyah returned and offered the Cherokee the gift of his alphabet. It was the first system ever invented for writing an Indian language. Because his symbols were based on sounds, children could learn to write in days. Within a few years, thousands of Cherokee could read and write in their own language.

By 1827 the Cherokee had produced their own written Constitution, based on that of the United States, declaring themselves a self-governing nation. It was printed in their own weekly newspaper, the *Cherokee Phoenix*. Then, in 1832, the Cherokee took the U.S. government to the Supreme Court and won the legal right to their lands.

The Trail of Tears

The Cherokee were a nation of farmers who could read and write. Yet President Jackson forced them from their land.

▲ The Cherokee wanted an Indian state to be named after Sequoyah. Instead, his name was given to the great redwood tree—sequoia.

◀ A painting of Sequoyah showing the Cherokee alphabet he invented

PARK HILL:
on Press. John Candy, Printer.
1845.

▲ A schoolbook from 1845, printed in the Cherokee language

In the winter of 1838, 15,000 Cherokees were driven at gunpoint into camps. They were then forced to march 1,200 miles (2,000 km) to Indian Territory. During the journey, 4,000 of them died. One of the accompanying soldiers called it "the cruelest work I ever knew." The Cherokee called it simply the Trail of Tears.

In 1843, Sequoyah died in Mexico. The letter sent to Indian Territory announcing his death was written in his own Cherokee language.

SEQUOYAH'S ALPHABET

Sequoyah's alphabet contained 86 symbols, each one representing a spoken syllable. The system was so simple that there was no need for teachers and missionaries—the Cherokee could teach it to each other.

POCAHONTASKING PHILIPTECUMSEH**SEQUOYAH**SACAGAWEACHIEF JOSEPHGERONIMOCRAZY HORSESITING BULL

Native Americans in the Time of Sacagawea

BEFORE THE nineteenth century, the many Indian peoples who lived around the central plains of America had not really been affected by the growing European settlements. The United States had spread out along the eastern coast. To the west lay a vast area of unmapped land.

Until 1803, the land west of the Mississippi had been claimed by France. Under the Louisiana Purchase, the French now sold it to the United States for $15 million. Europeans knew little about this wilderness. Wild rumors told of unicorns, pygmy tribes, and fields of gold. President Thomas Jefferson was determined to explore it and find a route all the way to the Pacific Ocean.

▲ An engraving from a book of 1812, showing Lewis and Clark talking with Native Americans during their famous expedition

On May 14, 1804, an expedition of thirty people, led by Meriwether Lewis and William Clark, headed up the Missouri River into the unknown. Their journey would last over two years. Just as Pocahontas had helped Europeans to conquer the East, now a Native American woman named Sacagawea would help them discover the West.

◄ A map showing the route of the Lewis and Clark expedition

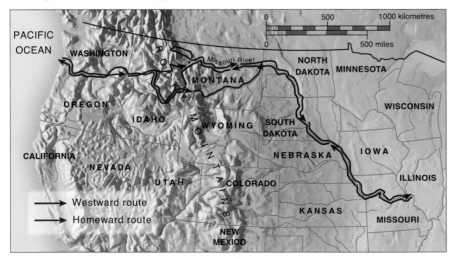

SACAGAWEA

Guide
circa 1786 to 1884

Lewis and Clark spent the winter of 1804 in a camp near a village of Hidatsa Indians. There they hired a guide, an old French Canadian fur trapper named Toussaint Charbonneau. He was accompanied by his young Indian wife, Sacagawea, or "Bird Woman."

CRADLEBOARDS

Sacagawea was able to take her baby on the expedition because of the excellent design of Indian baby carriers. Babies were often strapped into beaded buckskin pouches attached to beautiful cradleboards. A baby could then be carried safely on its mother's back or attached to the saddle of a horse.

Sacagawea was born among the Shoshone, who lived far to the northwest. As a girl, she had been captured by Hidatsa warriors. Charbonneau had then "won" her in a gambling game. Sacagawea gave birth to a son in February 1805. Nevertheless, she joined the expedition when it set off in April—with her baby, Jean-Baptiste, in a cradleboard on her back.

◄ Sacagawea guiding the American explorers. Around her shoulders is the strap of her son's cradleboard.

SPOTLIGHT ON SACAGAWEA

Indian Name:	Sacagawea
English Name:	Bird Woman
People:	Shoshone
Position:	Guide, interpreter
Born:	About 1786, in present-day Idaho
Died:	1884, Wind River Shoshone Reservation, in Wyoming
They Said:	[Sacagawea had] "borne with a patience truly admirable the fatigues of so long a route, encumbered with the charge of an infant." (William Clark)

Journey to the Pacific Ocean

To the explorers, Sacagawea soon proved to be more valuable than her husband. She dug up roots for them to eat, in the traditional Native American way. When her husband panicked and overturned a canoe, she calmly rescued the expedition's medical and scientific equipment. The explorers recognized her bravery by naming a waterway Bird Woman River after her.

Reaching the Rocky Mountains, the explorers met Shoshone warriors, among them Sacagawea's own brother. Meeting the Europeans made the Shoshone nervous, but Sacagawea made sure the expedition could pass peacefully. She was also able to obtain precious horses and guides. Farther west, the expedition met with Nez Percé Indians, and Clark wrote how once again Sacagawea acted as a "token of peace."

FLATTENED HEADS

Lewis and Clark made notes about many Indian customs. One of the most striking was the Chinook's practice of strapping their babies into cradleboards with a second board pressing on the skull. This gave adult Chinooks long, flattened foreheads, which they considered beautiful.

▼ This photograph of a Shoshone woman was taken later in the nineteenth century, but it shows clearly how Sacagawea would have carried Jean-Baptiste.

In November 1805, the group reached the Pacific Ocean. Sacagawea insisted on joining the party that explored the shore, so that she could see the whales, which she called "monstrous fish." Sacagawea guided Lewis and Clark safely home in 1806. They had mapped a route to the Pacific Ocean, discovered over 200 plant species and 100 animals, and met 50 Native American nations.

Sacagawea, who became a legend for her part in one of the greatest journeys in history, lived to be almost a hundred. She also lived to see the unfortunate effects her journey had on her people. Just as in the East, the first explorers in the West were soon followed by settlers, missionaries, and soldiers. They would claim the Shoshone's homeland as their own.

◀ A young descendant of Sacagawea attends her famous ancestor's grave on the Wind River Reservation, in Wyoming.

Native Americans in the time of Chief Joseph

BY THE mid-1800s, having reached the Pacific Coast, the Americans could no longer push the Native Americans farther west. Instead, they forced Indian peoples to sign treaties allowing the Indians to keep a part of their land, called a reservation. Europeans were allowed to settle on the rest.

The Nez Percé lived in the beautiful valleys of western Idaho and Oregon. In Lewis and Clark's footsteps, fur trappers called "mountain men" arrived there, and missionaries followed not far behind. In 1840 the Reverend Henry Spalding baptized the baby who would become Chief Joseph.

The number of Europeans grew, but for many years the Nez Percé proudly claimed that none were ever harmed by their people. In 1855, fifty-eight chiefs signed a treaty at Walla Walla. It promised the Nez Percé ownership of much of their traditional homeland, including the Wallowa Valley, forever.

▲ Before a meeting, Nez Percé chiefs smoked this peace pipe so that their words might be carried up on the smoke to the Sacred Powers.

BLACK KETTLE

Like Joseph, Black Kettle of the Cheyenne wanted to live in peace with the Americans. In 1864, a year after the "Thief Treaty" was signed, soldiers attacked his camp at Sand Creek. He had the Stars and Stripes and a white flag flying from his tipi when Colonel Chivington's troops attacked. The soldiers killed and scalped over 130 Cheyenne, most of them women and children.

CHIEF JOSEPH
Chief of the Nez Percé
1840 to 1904

In 1860, the Europeans discovered gold in the Wallowa Valley in Oregon, at Lapwai, near present-day Lewiston. Three years later, some Nez Percé chiefs, who did not even live there, were forced to sign a treaty giving away the Wallowa Valley. Old Chief Joseph refused to sign what he called the "Thief Treaty," and tore up his Bible. Just before his death, he made his son —who had grown into a fine chief—promise never to give up the land.

Young Chief Joseph made many speeches to the government, which promised that the Nez Percé could keep the Wallowa Valley. But gold diggers and settlers wanted the land. In May 1877, U.S. General Oliver Howard arrived and ordered Joseph to take his people to the reservation. When some of his young warriors killed four settlers, Joseph was forced to flee. He then led 700 men, women, and children on a historic journey toward Canada, where they thought they would be safe.

▼ Chief Joseph was a striking chief, in both peace and war. His magnificent war shirt is fringed with ermine, and he wears his hair in the traditional Nez Percé style.

POCAHONTASKING PHILIPTECUMSEHSEQUOYAHSACAGAWEACHIEF JOSEPHGERONIMOCRAZY HORSESITTING BULL

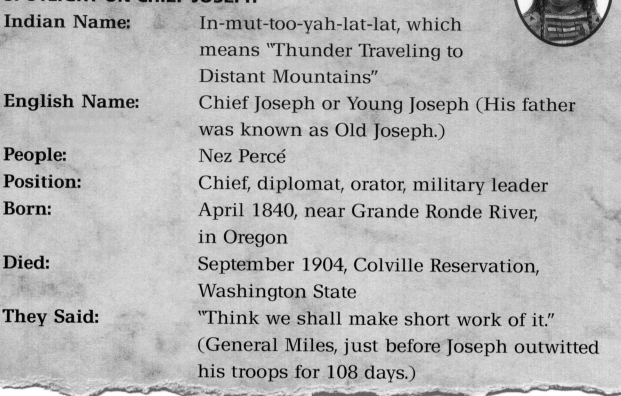

SPOTLIGHT ON CHIEF JOSEPH

Indian Name:	In-mut-too-yah-lat-lat, which means "Thunder Traveling to Distant Mountains"
English Name:	Chief Joseph or Young Joseph (His father was known as Old Joseph.)
People:	Nez Percé
Position:	Chief, diplomat, orator, military leader
Born:	April 1840, near Grande Ronde River, in Oregon
Died:	September 1904, Colville Reservation, Washington State
They Said:	"Think we shall make short work of it." (General Miles, just before Joseph outwitted his troops for 108 days.)

Flight of the Nez Percé

The Nez Percé were chased by four of America's top generals, with 2,000 troops. Yet they used their knowledge of the mountains to somehow escape capture. On one occasion Joseph's band passed straight over an army blockade. A soldier remembered: "Upon looking up, we discovered the Indians passing along the side of the cliff, where we thought a goat could not pass, much less an entire tribe of Indians."

In freezing October, after a battle in which Joseph's brother Ollokot was killed, the Nez Percé finally surrendered. They had traveled an amazing 1,700 miles (2,740 km) in eleven weeks, and were 40 miles (65 km) from Canada. Only seventy-nine warriors remained alive.

CHIEF JOSEPH'S SURRENDER

The famous speech Joseph made when he surrendered in 1877 captured the sadness felt by many Native Americans as they realized their battle could not be won: "I want to have time to look for my children and see how many of them I can find. Maybe I shall find them among the dead. Hear me, my chiefs! I am tired; my heart is sick and sad. From where the sun now stands I will fight no more forever."

▼ Nez Percé chiefs photographed in traditional costume on their reservation in 1906

◄ Chief Joseph in about 1880. He was a magnificent-looking man, who defended his people's lands with courage and dignity.

Joseph's people were moved to Fort Leavenworth, a reservation in Kansas, where more than twenty of them died of malaria. In the following years, Joseph met with three different presidents, and asked again and again if he might return to his beloved Wallowa Valley. No one would listen. When he died in Washington State in 1904, the doctor gave the cause of death as "a broken heart."

Native Americans in the Time of Geronimo

AS EUROPEAN settlers and traders took land in the West, the United States continued to grow. The United States went to war with Mexico, and in 1848 claimed lands including Texas, California, Arizona, and New Mexico. The U.S. government now had huge new areas to rule, lands that Mexico had not managed to control before. These lands were home to 7,000 Indians from a nation whose name had struck terror into the hearts of Mexicans for centuries—Apache!

The Apaches were able to survive in the dry, scorching deserts and rocky landscapes of Mexico and the southwestern United States. They lived by finding food and water in this barren land, and by raiding Mexican settlements. Their warriors were ferocious guerrilla fighters, who were almost impossible to capture. One American officer said that chasing the Apache was like "chasing deer with a brass band."

▼ Pioneers head west in 1866, through the mountains of California.

The United States wanted to force the Apaches onto reservations away from the new European settlements. They found this a frustrating task, not least with an Apache leader whose name became as famous as that of his people—Geronimo!

GERONIMO
Fighter and holy man
circa 1829 to 1909

▼ Geronimo, wearing a belt of
Spanish silver and his famous scowl

COCHISE

When the Butterfield Mail stagecoach began running
through Apache lands in 1858, Chief Cochise agreed to let it
pass safely through a route called Apache Pass. This
agreement ended in 1861, after an army lieutenant named
George Bascom captured and hanged the chief's brother and
nephew. In the following months, Cochise and Geronimo
killed some 150 Americans.

Geronimo and his band of followers fought bravely to avoid
living on a reservation. With his hawk's nose and piercing
eyes, Geronimo became a lasting symbol of the Native
Americans' struggle to remain free.

Geronimo's name came from the incident that made him
such a fearsome enemy. When he was a young warrior,
Mexican soldiers killed his mother, wife, and
children. In his grief, he saw a vision in which a
spirit told him he was bulletproof. He led a
revenge raid against the Mexicans, and
fought so fiercely that the soldiers
screamed "Geronimo!"—which was
Spanish for their Saint Jerome.

Geronimo spent the following years raiding
settlements with powerful chiefs such as
Cochise. But by the 1870s, the government had
succeeded in persuading many Apaches to settle
on various reservations. In 1877, Geronimo was
arrested and taken to San Carlos Reservation. Just like Chief
Joseph, he was expected to live a long way from home, on
land where crops would not grow.

31

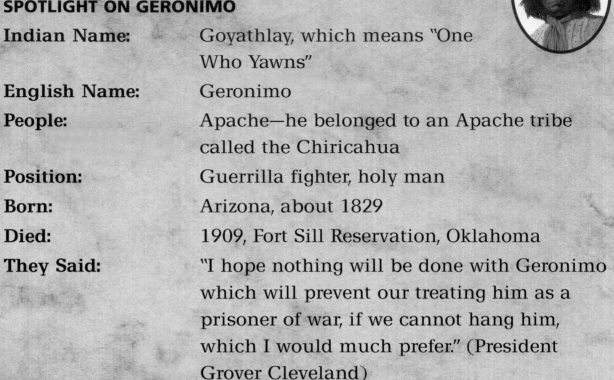

SPOTLIGHT ON GERONIMO

Indian Name:	Goyathlay, which means "One Who Yawns"
English Name:	Geronimo
People:	Apache—he belonged to an Apache tribe called the Chiricahua
Position:	Guerrilla fighter, holy man
Born:	Arizona, about 1829
Died:	1909, Fort Sill Reservation, Oklahoma
They Said:	"I hope nothing will be done with Geronimo which will prevent our treating him as a prisoner of war, if we cannot hang him, which I would much prefer." (President Grover Cleveland)

Fighting for freedom

Geronimo was not easily crushed. Three times, he escaped from San Carlos to terrify the settlers of the Southwest. On one occasion he came back to attack the reservation itself, and shot the Indian chief of police. The U.S. Army pursued him, but his small band vanished into the desolate landscape, until he chose to return.

In 1886, Geronimo made one last bid for freedom. He took only 38 followers, but such was his reputation that 5,000 soldiers lumbered after him. Even then, it was only by using Apaches as scouts that the soldiers finally tracked him down. Once again, the Indians found themselves fighting against their own people.

▲ A famous photograph of Geronimo discussing his surrender with General George Crook in 1886. You can see Geronimo's followers in the background.

RESERVATIONS

The Indian reservations were managed by the Bureau of Indian Affairs. Agents were appointed to hand out rations, but many of them cheated the Native Americans and sold part of the rations to make money. The Indians were expected to start farms, but the land was often very poor. Some signed up as Indian police or army scouts to make a living and avoid boredom.

▼ Geronimo wearing a top hat and driving a car on the Oklahoma reservation in 1908. His friends are posing for the photograph in their finest clothes.

After his surrender, Geronimo was imprisoned in Florida for two years, and then sent to a reservation far away in Oklahoma. He remained fiercely independent, and sold signed photographs to make money. Five years before his death, he was paraded in a Cadillac car at the 1904 St. Louis World's Fair. When an artist visited him on the reservation, Geronimo removed his shirt. He placed a pebble in each of the many bullet holes that marked his body. Making a sound like a gunshot, he whispered: "Crack! Bullets cannot kill me!"

Native Americans in the time of Crazy Horse

IN THE 1840s, thousands of pioneers set off to start a new life in the West. Farmers headed for the rich pastures of Oregon. Their wagon wheels carved a route across the United States that became known as the Oregon Trail. In 1849, miners known as "49ers" joined the rush west after gold was discovered in California. Surveyors followed them, marking paths for railroads and telegraph lines.

The pioneers traveled across the plains that were home to the Lakota, Cheyenne, Arapaho, and Crow. These peoples roamed over vast areas, hunting the buffalo that supplied their every need. Until now, the only Europeans they had seen were traders selling them horses and guns. Now, trains of wagons wheeled across their hunting grounds, scaring away the buffalo herds.

In 1851, 10,000 Indians gathered at Fort Laramie in the heart of the plains. They signed a treaty agreeing to let the American Army build forts on their lands. The Indians called the Oregon Trail the Holy Road, because the treaty said the travelers on it must not be touched.

▼ A memorial to Crazy Horse, being carved out of the Black Hills, South Dakota. If you look closely, you can see the figure's head at the top, and an outline of his horse's head marked in white.

CRAZY HORSE
**Fighter and holy man
1841 to 1877**

VISIONS

The Lakota Sioux believed that their world was filled with supernatural powers. As a boy approached manhood, he tried to receive a vision of these powers. To achieve this, he took sweat baths, forced himself to stay awake, stared at the sun, and often chopped off a finger joint. A powerful vision would reveal his medicine. This was a set of rituals, prayers, or objects that would guide and protect his life.

▼ Crazy Horse, dressed in the sacred clothes, feathers, and paint that protected him in battle

Crazy Horse was born into the Oglala, part of the Lakota nation of Sioux peoples. As a child he was known as "Curly." At thirteen, he set out on a vision quest, a ritual to seek help from the Sacred Powers. After fasting for three days, he saw a vision of a man fighting at the front of his warriors, with a hawk tied in his hair and lightning painted on his face. Dressed in this way, Curly would become a famous fighter. He showed the power of his vision by killing two Arapaho warriors, and his proud father gave him a new name— Crazy Horse.

When he was twenty-four, Crazy Horse became a "Shirt-Wearer," a chief with a special duty to protect his people. The year was 1865, and soldiers had arrived to drive the Oglala farther from the Holy Road. The following year Crazy Horse led a famous attack, in which eighty troops under Captain William J. Fetterman were killed.

SPOTLIGHT ON CRAZY HORSE

Indian Name:	Ta-sunko-witko
English Name:	Crazy Horse
People:	Oglala group of the Lakota nation
Position:	"Shirt-Wearer," fighter, holy man
Born:	About 1841, Rapid Creek, east of the Black Hills
Died:	September 6, 1877, murdered at Fort Robinson on the Red Cloud Reservation
They Said:	"Justly regarded as the boldest, bravest, and most skillful warrior in the whole Sioux nation." (Captain J. G. Bourke)

The battles of 1876

Crazy Horse now led the Lakota to their two greatest victories over the U.S. Army. After gold was discovered in the Black Hills, more soldiers arrived to drive Crazy Horse's people onto reservations. A thousand of these soldiers, led by General Crook, were defeated at the Battle of the Rosebud by Cheyenne and Lakota warriors. They were led by Crazy Horse, screaming: "Today is a good day to die!"

A week later, on June 25, 1876, George Armstrong Custer's 7th Cavalry attacked a huge Indian camp at the Little Bighorn. Crazy Horse's warriors fought back furiously, killing every one of Custer's 215 men. One Indian warrior said of Crazy Horse: "All the soldiers were shooting at him, but he was never hit."

► A warrior's medicine bundle. After receiving a vision of an eagle, a warrior wore this charm made from eagle talons to seek the protection of the Sacred Powers.

CHIEF PLENTY COUPS

At the Battle of the Rosebud, General Crook was saved by warriors from the Crow people, including Chief Plenty Coups. Just as Crazy Horse had received a vision showing how to fight the Europeans, Plenty Coups had received a vision showing him that the buffalo and the Indian way of life would soon disappear. This was why he fought on the side of the U.S. soldiers.

▼ Native Americans recorded historical events using pictures called "pictographs." This one shows Custer being killed by a warrior with a lance.

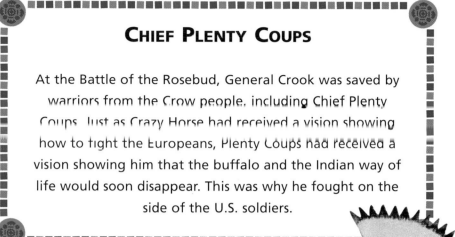

▼ A Chicago newspaper from July 6, 1876 reports the killing of Custer's command.

The following year, Crazy Horse saw that his people were exhausted and hungry. On May 6, 1877, he finally surrendered at the Red Cloud Reservation. Painted for war, Crazy Horse rode at the head of 900 followers, all of them singing. One officer commented: "By God! This is a triumphal march, not a surrender!"

Native Americans in the time of Sitting Bull

BY THE mid-1870s, the few American settlers of Pocahontas's time had grown to 40 million people. Sitting Bull said his people had become "an island of Indians in a lake of whites."

Government treaties squeezed the Indians into ever smaller reservations. Red Cloud, who had led the war in which Crazy Horse's warriors wiped out Fetterman's command, was settled on a reservation two years later. He said of the government: "They made us many promises, more than I can remember, but they never kept but one. They promised to take our land, and they took it."

As the chiefs surrendered, they had to learn how to live on the reservations. For some it was impossible—Crazy Horse was murdered within months of his surrender. For Sitting Bull, it was another opportunity to defy the Europeans.

▲ The Oglala chiefs Red Cloud (right) and American Horse (left), photographed on the reservation in 1891

THE BUFFALO

Sitting Bull's name came from his father's vision of a sacred buffalo. The Lakota Sioux ate the buffalo's meat, made its hide into tipis and clothes, and used its dung for fuel. When European hunters began killing buffalo for their hides and leaving the meat to rot, the Indians knew their old life could not continue. There had once been 30 million buffalo, but by 1886 fewer than 1,000 animals were left.

SITTING BULL

**Chief and holy man
1831 to 1890**

Sitting Bull was born into the Hunkpapa group of the Lakota Sioux. He was given his name at the age of fourteen, after showing great bravery in a battle with the Crow nation. It was a sacred name given by his father, a holy man, who had received it in a medicine vision of the buffalo.

As he grew into a skillful warrior and chief of the Hunkpapa, Sitting Bull received many of his own visions. He once demonstrated his medicine in a battle with soldiers who had accompanied surveyors into Lakota Sioux lands. Sitting Bull sat out in the open and calmly smoked his pipe, while the soldiers' bullets flew around him. Like Geronimo, he seemed to be bulletproof.

Before Custer's attack in 1876, some 15,000 Indians had been attracted to Sitting Bull's camp by the chief's medicine. There, Sitting Bull performed a Sun Dance ceremony. One hundred pieces of flesh were cut from his arms before he danced and stared at the sun. A powerful vision came. It showed dead soldiers falling into the camp "like grasshoppers." The Indians believed this vision made their victory at the Little Bighorn certain.

◄ Sitting Bull, whose powerful medicine was at the heart of the Native Americans' resistance

SPOTLIGHT ON SITTING BULL

Childhood Name:	Hunkesni, which means "Slow"
Adult Name:	Tatanka Iyotake, which means "Sitting Bull"
People:	Hunkpapa group of the Lakota Sioux
Position:	Holy man, chief
Born:	About 1831, Grand River, South Dakota
Died:	Murdered by Indian police, December 14, 1890
They Said:	"He had a big brain and a good one, a strong heart and a generous one." (An old warrior remembering Sitting Bull)

The last great chief surrenders

Even after Crazy Horse gave up the impossible fight in 1877, Sitting Bull led his followers north to Canada. For four years, they lived and hunted there. But the buffalo were dying out as quickly as the Indians. In 1881 Sitting Bull headed south, and became the last of the chiefs to surrender. His great camp on the Little Bighorn had been reduced to 185 people.

Sitting Bull was held as a prisoner of war for two years. Buffalo Bill had him released for a while so that he could join his Wild West show. Then Sitting Bull was settled on the Standing Rock Reservation, where he continued to defy the Europeans. When officials arrived to open a new railroad, Sitting Bull was chosen to welcome them. He spoke in Lakota Sioux, and only the interpreter knew that as he smiled he was saying: "You are thieves and liars. You have taken away our land and made us outcasts."

In 1890, the Ghost Dance religion spread across the reservations. Sitting Bull was falsely accused of using it to stir unrest. Three years before, Indian police had held Crazy Horse's arms as he was murdered by a soldier. Now, in the winter of 1890, Indian policemen in their government uniforms shot and killed Sitting Bull. It was a familiar tragic ending in the life of a great Native American.

▲ Followers of the Ghost Dance wore brightly decorated shirts and dresses like this one, to perform the sacred dance.

◄ Sitting Bull and Buffalo Bill Cody in 1885. By joining Buffalo Bill's Wild West Show, Sitting Bull was able to travel away from the reservation.

GHOST DANCE

The Ghost Dance religion was started by the Paiute shaman Wovoka during an eclipse. Wovoka promised a return of the dead Indians and the buffalo, but he urged his followers to behave peacefully. The U.S. authorities became alarmed when many Sioux joined the religion, so the army crushed the Ghost Dance movement.

▲ Wovoka, the Paiute shaman who started the Ghost Dance religion

Different Lives

IN 1890, the Indians began to dance. The shuffling steps and sacred songs of the Ghost Dance brought visions of the days before the Europeans. The visions brought hope that those days might return. In the end, however, they brought one more tragedy. In December 1890, troops gunned down more than 150 Lakota Sioux Ghost Dancers at the camp of Chief Big Foot. This was the Massacre of Wounded Knee, and it marked the end of the armed struggle against the settlers.

The old Indian way of life, which had produced the historic lives of Pocahontas, Tecumseh, Geronimo, and Sitting Bull, came to an end. Yet the twentieth century produced its own Native Americans who made history. Jim Thorpe, of the Sauk and Fox nation, was one of the most famous U.S. athletes. At the 1912 Stockholm Olympics, he became the first man to win the gold medal in both the pentathlon and decathlon. During World War II, Navajo "Code Talkers" successfully used their own language to send radio messages so that the Japanese would not be able to understand them.

► Native American families, like this one pictured in a photographer's Idaho studio, had to learn a new way of life on the reservations.

Until the 1930s, government schools banned Native American children from learning their own languages and religions. But Native Americans carried on the struggle to protect their remaining lands and preserve their languages and traditions. In 1991, members of the Sisseton-Wahpeton Sioux from North Dakota took back the bones of their ancestors, which had been kept in a Washington museum. Giving these remains a proper burial, one member of the nation said: "We see this as the beginning of a journey of recovery . . . a recovery of honor, dignity, and honesty."

▼ Today, there are about 1,800,000 Native Americans living in the United States, on reservations that cover about 32,000 square miles (83,000 sq km). Many Native Americans take pride in their traditional clothing, culture, and customs.

◄ This famous photograph from World War II shows Private Ira Hayes (left), a Pima Indian, helping to raise the Stars and Stripes during the defeat of the Japanese on the island of Iwo Jima.

Time line

c.12,000 B.C.	Native Americans first arrive on the North American continent.
A.D. 1492	Columbus "discovers" America.
c.1595	Pocahontas is born.
1607	English settlers found Jamestown.
1617	Pocahontas dies.
1620	The Pilgrim Fathers land at Plymouth.
1621	A treaty is signed between the Plymouth colony and the Wampanoags.
c.1638	King Philip is born.
1675–1676	King Philip's War
1676	King Philip is killed.
c.1760	Sequoya is born.
1763	Pontiac leads an uprising against the British.
1768	Tecumseh is born.
1783	America wins independence from Britain.
c.1786	Sacagawea is born.
1803	The Louisiana Purchase. The United States buys land in the West from France.
1804–1806	The Lewis and Clark expedition
1813	Tecumseh is killed at the Battle of the Thames.
1821	Sequoya gives the Cherokees an alphabet.
c.1829	Geronimo is born.
1830	The Indian Removal Act is passed.
c.1831	Sitting Bull is born.
1838	The Trail of Tears—Cherokees are forced to move to Indian Territory.
1840	Chief Joseph is born.
c.1841	Crazy Horse is born.
1843	Sequoya dies.
1848	The United States claims land in the Southwest after war with Mexico.
1849	Miners flock to California in the gold rush.
1851	Many chiefs of the plains peoples sign a treaty at Fort Laramie.
1855	Nez Percé chiefs sign a treaty at Walla Walla.

1858	Cochise agrees to let the Butterfield Mail coach pass through Apache Pass.
1863	Some Nez Percé chiefs are forced to sign a treaty giving away the Wallowa Valley.
1864	Black Kettle's Cheyenne followers are massacred at Sand Creek.
1876	The battles of the Rosebud and the Little Bighorn.
1877	Chief Joseph leads his people on their flight toward Canada. Crazy Horse is killed.
1881	Sitting Bull surrenders.
1884	Sacagawea dies.
1886	Geronimo breaks out of the reservation for the last time.
1887	The Dawes Act breaks up reservations into individual plots of land, allowing settlers to take any unclaimed land.
1890	The Ghost Dance religion spreads. Sitting Bull is killed. Chief Big Foot's followers are massacred at Wounded Knee.
1904	The death of Chief Joseph
1909	Geronimo dies.
1912	Native American Jim Thorpe wins Olympic gold in the pentathlon and decathlon.
1934	The Indian Reorganization Act reverses the 1887 policy, and encourages landholding and self-government, improved education, and religious freedom for Indian nations.
1942–1945	Native Americans play an important role in the war effort of the United States.
1973	Two Native Americans are shot and killed at Wounded Knee during a protest by the American Indian Movement against the breaking of treaties.
1991	Members of the Sisseton-Wahpeton Sioux nation take back the bones of their ancestors.

Glossary

blockade   A barrier to keep an enemy from getting through.

breechcloth   Loincloth. A cloth worn around the hips or loins.

colony   A group of settlers in a new country.

creation myths   Stories telling how a people first came to live in the world.

guerrillas   Small groups of fighters moving quickly and using surprise raids against a regular army.

heathens   A term used for people who were not Christians, Jews, or Muslims.

missionaries   People sent by a Church to spread its faith.

moccasin   Native American shoe.

papoose   A young child.

pioneer   One of the first people to settle in a new land.

prophets   Religious leaders who predict future events.

pygmy   A traditional people who were very short.

ransack   To attack a place and search through it in order to steal goods.

reservation   An area of land, usually of poor quality, where Native Americans were forced to live.

sachem   The supreme chief of some Native American nations.

Sacred Powers   The spirits and gods the Indians believed guided their world.

scalped   Cut away hair and skin from the heads of dead people as a trophy.

squaw   Offensive word for a Native American wife or woman.

stagecoach   A horse-drawn coach that carried passengers regularly along different routes.

surrender   To give up the fight.

telegraph   A machine for sending messages.

tipi   A tent made from poles and skins—used by Native Americans on the plains.

unicorn   A mythical horse with a horn, spoken of in stories.

waterway   A river or channel of water.

wigwam   A tent or hut of bark or skins used by American Indians of the northeast.

Further information

Books to read

Blackhawk, Ned. *The Shoshono*. Raintree Steck-Vaughn, 2000.

Green, Carl R. *Sacagawea: Native American Hero*. Enslow, 1997.

Guttmacher, Peter. *Crazy Horse: Sioux War Chief*. Chelsea House, 1994.

Hermann, Spring. *Geronimo: Apache Freedom Fighter*. Enslow, 1997.

McAmis, Herb. *The Cherokee*. Raintree Steck-Vaughn, 2000.

Viola, Herman J. *North American Indians: An Introduction to the Lives of America's Native Peoples, from the Inuit of the Arctic to the Zuni of the Southwest*. Crown Publishers, 1996.

Websites

http://www.si.edu/cgi-bin/nav.cgi
This site allows you to see the exhibits in the National Museum of the American Indian in New York.

http://www3.pbs.org/weta/thewest/wpages/wpgs000/w010_001.htm
This site, created by American documentary filmmakers, contains a number of biographies of Native American leaders.

Index

Figures in **bold** are illustrations.

Algonquian 7
alphabet, Cherokee 20, 21, **21**
Apache 30, 31, 32

Battle of the Little Bighorn 36
Battle of the Rosebud 36, 37
Battle of the Thames 17
Black Kettle 26
buffalo 38
Buffalo Bill 40, **40**

Charbonneau, Toussaint 23
Cherokee 18, 19, 20, 21
chiefs 5, 10, **29**
Christianity 9, 10, 11
Cochise, Chief 31
Columbus, Christopher 4
cradleboards 23, 25, **25**
Crazy Horse 34, 35, **35**, 36, 37, 38
Crook, General George **32**, 36, 37
Custer, General George Armstrong 36, 37, **37**

Fort Laramie, Treaty of 34

Geronimo 30, 31, **31**, 32, **32**, 33, **33**
Ghost Dance religion 40, 41
gold rush 34

Harrison, William Henry 15, 16, **16**
Hayes, Ira **43**

Hidatsa 23
Hunkpapa 39, 40

Indian Removal Act 18, 19

Jackson, President Andrew 18, 20
Jamestown colony 6, **6**, 7, 8, 9
Jefferson, President Thomas 22
Joseph, Chief 26, 27, **27**, 28, **28**, 29

King Philip's War 12, 13

Lakota Sioux 34, 35, 36, 39, 40, 41
Lalawethika *see* Tenskwatawa
Lewis and Clark expedition 22, **22**, 23, 24, 25
Louisiana Purchase 22

Massacre of Wounded Knee 42
Massasoit, Chief 10
medicine bundle **36**
Mexico and Mexicans 30, 31
missionaries 9, 10, 11, 26
Mugg, Rogue 13

Nez Percé 24, 26, 27, 28, 29, **29**

Oregon Trail 34

peace pipe **26**
Philip, King 10, 11, **11**, 12, 13
pirates 13
Plenty Coups, Chief 37
Plymouth colony 10, 11

Pocahontas 6, 7, **7**, 8, 9, **9**
Pontiac 17
Powhatan, Chief 7, 8
praying towns 10, 11
Prophet's Town 15, 16
prophets 14

Red Cloud 38, **38**
reservations 26, 29, **29**, 30, 31, 32, 33, 38, 43, **43**
Rolfe, John 8

Sacagawea 22, 23, **23**, 24, 25
Seminole 19
sequoia tree **20**
Sequoyah 18, 19, **19**, 20, 21, **21**
Shawnee 14, 15, 16, 17
Shoshone 23, 24, 25, **25**
Sitting Bull 38, 39, **39**, 40, **40**, 41
Smith, Captain John 6, 7
Squanto 9, 10
Sun Dance ceremony 39

Tecumseh 14, 15, **15**, 16, 17, **17**
Tenskwatawa 14, 15, 16
Thorpe, Jim 42
Trail of Tears 20, 21

Virginia 6, **6**
visions 35, 36, 37, 39

Wallowa Valley 26, 27
Wampanoag 9, 10, 11, 12, 13
wampum **10**, 11, 15
Wovoka 41, **41**